D0868457

Terms and Conditions

Terms and Conditions

Tania Hershman

Nine
Arches
Press

Terms and Conditions
Tania Hershman

ISBN: 978-1-911027-22-5

Copyright © Tania Hershman, 2017

Cover artwork: 'Pleasures Called Pitch' © Hollie Chastain
www.holliechastain.com

All rights reserved. No part of this work may be reproduced, stored or transmitted in any form or by any means, graphic, electronic, recorded or mechanical, without the prior written permission of the publisher.

Tania Hershman has asserted her right under Section 77 of the Copyright, Designs and Patents Act 1988 to be identified as the author of this work.

First published July 2017 by:

Nine Arches Press
PO Box 6269
Rugby
CV21 9NL
United Kingdom

www.ninearchespress.com

Printed in the United Kingdom by Imprint Digital

Nine Arches Press is supported using public funding by the National Lottery through Arts Council England.

Supported using public funding by
**ARTS COUNCIL
ENGLAND**

for Jo

Contents

iii. privacy policy

i. data collection

Baby

for Helen

Baby travels
trains, collecting
faces. (Baby may seem

carried, but is, in fact,
directing.) Baby takes in
all ages, colours,

male, female,
other. Baby understands
the need for data.

Baby's favourite
is the oldest: its valleys,
shades and loose-pinned

edges. When Baby is removed
there are thoughts
of screaming. Instead

Baby scrolls through
images amassed. One day,
thinks Baby, I will not be

so smooth, so new. Let me
be old, prays Baby. Let me not
be carried. Let me wait

alone on dark platforms,
knowing and not knowing where
or why I'm going.

1 & 2

1.

Catch me, appled, love, oh catch me. Dimpled, I am sweeter, loves of honey, men and ministries. You talk me, peached; I sink. And sinking, trip. I fly. Summon me troops, warn me whispered, take me longing, fighting, sleepless.

2.

Night will come and then the night will come and then the rain. The night comes, rained, and you are more night to my rain, darkened we are only shuttered, and after dark. And after.

Advice for the traveller

Fall, if possible
within an hour of your arrival

in any new city. Fall well
on knees and hands, in public,

make sure you are seen. Bleeding
is optional. If someone immediately

lifts you without pausing
his mobile conversation, you will know

this is a place worth staying in. Limp
to the nearest park, sit and watch

locals by a fountain, dozing, kissing,
walking dogs. Do not rush. If you have

fallen properly, there will be no need
to fall here again. Your knee's sweet

sting and bruise will remind you
of attention, the necessity for kindness.

All their hands

The mothers
and the daughters
standing
side by side.

A wind
catches their hair;
all their hands
go up at once.

The mothers
and the daughters
sigh.

The mothers
reach out
for their daughters.

The field is empty. The wind
is only air.

What do we do when the water rises?

Fire ants, when flooded, make
of themselves a raft, hooking bodies;
when stranded, make of themselves

a bridge. And when a colony
is tipped into a bucket: sphere.

Scientists have tried
to persuade them
to disband, pushing

the ant architectures further
and further down
into the water, but where

a single ant will sink, together
they cling on. How do they know

how hard to hold, and when
to let each other go?

Life just swallows you up

Father dies during the appetizers. Mother
    keeps on eating. How's work? she says. I
        pour more wine. She passes

    just before dessert arrives. Shame,
        says the waiter, poised to whisk away
            her Eton Mess. Leave it, I say

        and sit there, orphaned, staring at both puddings,
            wondering how I am ever going
                to lift my spoon again.

Insist on it

Whatever it is they give you, insist on this one. Insist on this package with the red seal although they will offer green, they will press upon you magenta, they will want not to seal it at all. Do not accept, even if it is bound in thick paper that smells of exactly the spot from your childhood home in which you felt most alone and happy. Do not expect there to be any forward motion from them on any issue, it is only backwards with such people, ever stretching backwards to before your birth, they see so long, they see with those sorts of eyes and the kinds of minds that fold in on themselves. When you have it to hand, the package with the red seal, step out of the shop, step out without showing them the other side of your head, and then turn and run. Hold it in your hands and run fast.

Lessons in Flanders agriculture

Folding a field takes an army
        one man at each corner
                many down the sides

They bend   slide their hands beneath
        chalk and sod   lift   and run
                towards their comrades

When it is done   when the light is gone and the men
      are spent   there is no-one left
                to listen to the field   sighing

Dressing for flight

Give me a skirt with aeroplanes on it,
she whispered, fingering fabric, slipping
between rows of clothes. I want,
she murmured into the sleeves
of the hanging jacket with patches
of peaches, a skirt filled with Spitfires,
Hurricanes, dive-bombing. Slide me
under the waistband, show me
what heaven sounds like,
falling away.

And on

Perhaps your phone is off
or you are off
on trains and trains and buses, or you are off
me, a possibility I am always
considering, although I may be off
the mark, a phrase from the races, getting off
on the wrong foot, which we did, love
came later and then we were off
and running, who knows
what might happen next. There is a man

walking past my car, which I like
to keep an eye on from my window. He is
swaying, rhythm off,
and I am worried, love, that he will fall.
In my pyjamas, would I rush down, or hope
that someone else, or the man himself,
would lift him off
the ground so he might,
unsteady, carry on.

After you go

After you go, the house and I negotiate, all glass, forks and cookware. Moods I am in include: elation, cleanliness, obsession, tenderness, depression. I wipe counters. You, love, leave no stain, no mark, but books and books and t-shirts whispering in drawers, crushed pepper in the pestle – or the mortar, I was never sure. One thuds and smashes, while the other, stoic, holds its ground below.

The weight of us

As I line up to board my flight
I see the pilot

lean out and wipe his window
with what looks like

a tissue. Surrounded
by technology, I find this

reassuring: the man
charged with the weight

of us, trusting nothing
but his own hand.

The woman in the bath

At a certain point
she vanishes
and it becomes a soup
of limbs and liquid. She may
fall asleep, held
and floating. Yes, the womb. But
yes also now
control, over hot and
cold, choosing when
to step out, dry off
solidify.

The way walls do

We meet for our silent teas

in a café. There is cake, of course

and relief; I am free

to watch the china

bump your lower lip, note

the finger you pick

crumbs up with, feel

your gaze as I drink

my second cup. After an hour

we pay and leave. I'm sure

they talk about us

when we're gone.

But if I knew a little more

Bird. Bird after bird. Into and under. More birds. And then string. String pulling birds. I whistle and you. I whistle and you dive and flap and surrender.

Before breakfast, you leave me, again. I promise, you say, and I can hear the birds on your shoulders, in your pockets, skimming through your hair. You said that last time, I whisper, but you have already gone. The bird sitting opposite me shrugs. Sometimes, the bird seems to say, it's enough. It's just enough.

Interview with a wind turbine

Question One: Are you jealous of the tree, its roots,
                     its sap, its leaves?

Question Two: Are you winking at me?

Question Three: In what language do you cry, and
                     how do your sisters, cousins,
                     aunts reply?

Question Four: What would you like more:
                     to walk, to sweat, to sigh,
                     to close your eyes?

Question Five: When birds dive-bomb you,
                     do you laugh, or slice them
                     through?

Question Six: If I reached for your blade, would
                     you lift me to spin with you
                     forever in the wind?

Answer One: What is a tree but some version which better breathes?

Answer Two: Do you want me to be?

Answer Three: These are words I don't know, I don't cry, they do not reply.

Answer Four: I have no need to move, but would like to sleep, to sigh, to know love.

Answer Five: They come like everything from the sky, and I am sorry we can't have more time.

Answer Six: Stretch, just a little further, yes.

The bed

is queen-size   a gift
from me to myself   The queen
is wider than the king   That side
I use for storage   spare pillow
a dozen t-shirts   pyjamas
socks   not in
case of need   but to have
within reach   those that also know
the neck   the cheek
the push   of chest
a shoulder's edge   and slide
of skin   our hearts
lift   and yield

Kiss, the first

First, the
    kiss, I have
        imagined it and
         imagined it
           over and
              again

Kiss, a film of it,
    rewind and play
        the same two
           sets of lips meet
           over and
              again

                again and
                  over, meet
                    lips of sets, two
                      same the play-and-rewind-it
                    of film:
                      a kiss

                again and
                  over
                    it imagined and it
                      imagined: have I?
                        Kiss the first.

What the choreographer knows about flight

Early humans used to sleep
in trees, and our nightmares
of falling may be some
ancient protective mechanism
beds have not yet overridden.
The choreographer calls her dancers
action heroes, has them fall
and fall and fall again. I wonder
how I might feel
at one of her performances.
Relieved not to be
plummeting myself from twenty,
thirty feet? Or reminded
of those forest nights, spine
pressed into the branches,
no thought of beneath.

ii. warranties & disclaimers

Today we have no forecast

This heat was not expected
as soldiers are not expected
as rain is expected
as some babies are expected
as that lost parcel is
      never expected to arrive
and you are not expected
to come tonight, but I
sit here anyway, heart
wide open, not expecting
everything.

Led astray by evidence

Scientists had assumed
rising ocean acidity
would be harmful
to coral reefs. Now
they find them thriving.
I had thought myself
flimsy, easily undone
by missing you. These
are questions, say the scientists,
we have no answers to.

And what we know about time

When it failed to alarm, my father
took the clock apart. Laid it
all out on the kitchen table. While the dog
dreamed and snored, we watched him
clean every piece, then, with breaths held,
attempt reassembly. It worked

perfectly for the next ten years, which was odd,
given the sixteen horological components
my father couldn't fit back in. (They
lived out their days in that kitchen drawer
designated for such things.)

There must have been someone, somewhere,
now – like my father, like the dog,
the kitchen table and that drawer –
long gone, who once knew
exactly what those sixteen parts were for.

How the world doesn't work

The child
who tried
to steal

a chess piece
from the sets
set out

on the street
as if
for anyone

       and, crying,
       was made
       to return it

will not
in later years
become

a chess champion.

What we don't know we do not know

Come now, says a voice from a corner   **you can't see me**   I can't see.
Do you think bright   **shiny shiny**   is the way it's meant   **by some**
great deity   to be? Oh no, this gauzy film   **what a relief**   which does
unviolence to your   **poor and tired**   eyes, lifts
the weight   **so much to see**   of information, objects
shifting   **here and there they are**   at the whim
of   **new fangled**   bulb or   **good old**   candle. This
uncertainty   **who knows anything for sure**   is our new
reference frame. Do purchase   **for a large amount**   and read
the handbook if you will,   **life moves too fast**
for handbooks   but remember:
the instructions   **that you crave**
are liable to   **dance always and forever**   change.

The medical student comes to talk to me about her ethics essay

She cries. Not, I think,
because her assignment
involves a dilemma (fictional)
in which a child might die,
but because up to this point
she has skated coolly
on facts, and is now being asked
to dive. She feels, I think,
that she can only fail. Be
brave, I say, but who am I
to give advice?

No, I do not tango

Don't call for me there, I have stepped
off that dance floor, and I am

relieved. Every part of me
is mine, no hand on my shoulder, arm

around my waist, no waiting
for an invitation. A hundred years ago

they would have called me – with those
two million others – surplus, extra. Elizabeth

the First caused similar confusion. No mate,
no children. Virgin Queen, they also named her

Mother of the Nation. Also: Prince. You
can call me anything you like. I know my name.

Mirrors must not be

We are not symmetrical, heart to the left, appendix off centre, and you will see one of my ears, if you look closely, is unlike, and my hair falls more one way and will not be retrained. We are not spheres, nor billiard balls, and mirrors must not be trusted. We are programmed, they tell us, to assess each other's faces half by half, and if one certain half is beautiful, then so's the whole, especially women to men. O evolution, you look at us sideways, slant. Is my half-face, the face I turn to you, why you say you love me? Or, would it be true with your eyes shut, my eyes shut too?

Some nature is binding

She does not expect to be recognised
from one occasion to the next, feels
her face easily forgotten, is amazed
when not only her but something she's said
is remembered. This chips away at her
conviction of insignificance, but *ohsoslowly*

like the ancient lichen which grows one centimetre
every hundred years. She suspects neither of them
can change shape or pace, or let go
of what they cling to.

Terms and Conditions

I can't call it mine, though I paint its nails my chosen shades,
I clean and feed it. Mostly, it seems satisfied; sometimes
I'm woken in the night, stomach complaining.
It sits me on this sofa, walks me to work.
Is the agreement hire-purchase?
Or am I a hotel guest:
sure, make a mess, we'll straighten the sheets – but don't
            stealfromtheminibar smashamirror riptheTVfromthewall
                              We have your credit card.
When I vacate, who next gets that tiny kettle, the unused
shampoos? Will I regret
leaving the miniatures untouched?
And will my final sigh be for the fear
that wouldn't let me ignore prudence and warning letters,
                              turn the volume up
                                  and roar.

Unforgotten

Her son calls her the human calendar –
any date and she will tell you
where she was, with whom, and even,
decades later, what she wore. But he doesn't know

how she also recalls the very hour
of the very night she began to long, with shame,
for the blanket of dementia,
the feathered ecstasy of now.

Keeping watch

I wake up from a dream in which
I am going quickly blind. I wake up
still spinning from the fall

of darkness, that pinhole
closing in. Rarely has a dream felt
so concrete. I had gone to sleep certain

my new philosophy on life could help me
weather anything. Clearly, my subconscious
did not approve. That primitive

survival urge which prefers us always
fearful, alert. Well, I refuse. I will not. Here
comes another night. Bring it on.

Undetected

You say you left, but I'm not sure. You say, Have it all, I'm off. But I think you're still here. I look for you under tiles, between sofa cushions. I let the light in as if you might be between the particles. I sweep and sweep the floor, and you may be dust, microscopic. Will I need instruments to see you at ever-shrinking scales?

Days and hours and minutes and I am unconvinced. I feel you, I hear you – although what you say to me is that you've gone, is that I'm an idiot, I'm wasting time. And you don't look at me the way you did.

I check everything again, pick up tiles and cushions, let light in, light out, clean the floor, and then I bend. Perhaps you're right, I say out loud. But we both know, and together we sit, with beams and cross-beams, neutrinos spinning through and through and through.

For which we have no names

She works one day a week
in a building which also houses
a Centre for Synaptic Plasticity,
and each time she sees the sign
she wants to go in and say,
Take my brain, bend it,
it's not behaving. She has

of late, and for no reason,
been *atrabilious*, a word
she learned recently
which sums up her state
perfectly: a mix
of irritability and melancholy.
Scientists have suggested

we can't feel emotions
we have no names for. This,
she thinks, is impossible
to prove. How do we know
what anyone means when they say *anger*,
when they say *jealousy*, when they say *love*?
She walks past the sign again, longing
to be wired up, explained. Who am I,
she'd say. Tell me my name.

My brilliant friend

You are not my rock   unless
  we both are rocks
and also soufflé   blancmange
  airy   shifting
volatile   We take turns
  to lean   here
is my shoulder   there is yours
  and catch   From the floor
we laugh   for what else is there
  to do but push over   roll up
look
  for stars

The time it takes to set

Not just that you didn't know
who I was

> after all our time together, but that you
> didn't try, weren't curious. I wanted you

to start sentences with *Because I know*
you love x or *y*, but it never happened

> so I left. Finding I didn't know
> myself, I melted

down the bronze, re-cast. I am still
liquid in parts, but oh, the light, the light.

Unhappened

No wife, no
husband, kids

unborn, no
holes torn

in socks, in sheets,
hotels un-

stayed, beach
sand unstirred, no

castles built, no
threats, no

smiles, no pubs
high in the hills, no
drinks rage-

spilled, no soft
all-mine other's hands, no

traveller exploring my unknown lands.

This is not my midnight

I am travel-spun   dazzled   and delighted

      when Ricardo steps out

from the bellboy pack   midnight-fresh

      and luggage-willing   Ricardo tells me

all I need to know about this city's

      oldest hotel   Here   says Ricardo

is the pool   and here

      the breakfast room   Ricardo

turns on my lights   heaves

the ungraceful case onto its perch   and leaves me

      time-drunk   on the king-size bed

the unviewed city sugar-ripe

      beyond the blackout curtains

iii. privacy policy

Missing you

The woman in her twenties
is amazed she's an anomaly. She's

doing fine – if fine means living,
breathing, getting married, having

children – without the chunk
that in us normals holds half

of all our neurons. Her brain,
the jaw-dropped doctors think,

became expert in alternatives,
workarounds, diversions. Who's to say

she's not finer than the rest
of us? Our signals

take no chances, walk
the roads most travelled by, while hers,

double-jointed,
                  are dancing.

Surplus, 1919

And what if you assembled them
in some giant stadium, all two million
and announced: We're very sorry

but there's no-one left
to marry you. Would there be outcry

demands for explanation, Why
did you send them? Thousands

upon thousands, and when they were gone
you dispatched reinforcements. Would they

charge the stage, commandeer the microphone, pitch you
to the crowds? Or sit, stunned, wondering

how now to live: alone
or worse, with parents; how

to earn, with what to occupy
those hours emptied of expected
spouse and children. And would they

still be sitting there, all two million
when you, impatient, having said

your piece, turn off
the lights, leave,
go home to your wife.

Beneath the cow

Beneath the cow, far far down, from the field behind and another thousand feet: a tunnel, made by men, to blow up other men. Beneath the cow, now so peaceful, now busy grazing, they ploughed through Belgian clay – during the dig, eleven perish, trapped, the twelfth surviving for six days to emerge, walk away from his grave, already dug.

And all this for what? A line of craters, now water-filled, lakes and pools, and inside these now one-hundred-year-old holes, alterations in Earth's geography, and history, their creators, tunnellers and sappers, heard for days afterwards their enemy crying. Men, buried, dying.

After seeing Monet's Waterlilies
and then hearing the news

I save a set of pores
for sadness (it's viscous,
sags the skin if you don't specify).
Usually I empty once a month,
or maybe
fortnightly
but now it's so much I can't keep up it spills into adjacent zones
where the walls are flimsy flooding is a real threat. I try
to activate the Emergency Heart Fence
but the button's stuck, instructions
shredded years ago. If you know how
to bail out, reinforce and stabilise
please call.

What is it that fills us

A song for the last of the gasometers

They first suggested relocation. They did this out of love,
wanting to avoid dismantlement, demolition. All but one
agreed; the final one said:
    – Not without my gas.

They went away, drew up plans and schemas, investigated
pressure, volume, temperature. They did this out of love.
But they had no solution.
    One of them went back alone and asked directly:

    – How – she said to the gas, which shifted so she
was never speaking to the same molecule twice – do we
move you? She waited, opened herself up. But all she heard
was whispering, hissing, as if the gas was suspicious.

She fell asleep. When she woke up, the gas, all the gas,
was gone. Then, the final one agreed to leave. Now they
stand empty in rows; each one of their hearts broken.

Body

I saw my mother's
heart today. She pressed
up against the machine
while, a few feet away
I watched it load
on the computer screen.
Is that...? I asked. The radiologist
immune to the novelty
of inside views, nodded.

I'd helped my mother
get undressed, seen
for the first time
the vest she wore
to cover where her breasts had been.
I had not expected
several minutes later
to see her chest –
like wings unfurling –
open itself out to me.

Released, my mother stood
small and grinning
in her backless gown,
not knowing what I'd seen
or what she'd shown.
I kept it to myself,
my mother's heart.
It had not looked
as I'd imagined, but
like a star, shooting
through her ribs, that body
I used to be a part of.

Relativity

You think there's a gap between us
You think we are separate   distinct
You think Newton had it right that we collide
       and come apart   collide
       and come apart   But
this is Einstein's world   A hundred
years ago   he showed how
we all are bound   I nudge space
      and you
      are shifted
You think if you're high enough
      you're safe   You think
when I fall   your orbit
      is unaltered   You think
this poem
      is just physics

Getting away with it

I want to be
the expert
in your rare condition.
I want to be the only
surgeon in the world
who knows how
to cut you open, stitch
you up. I want
to watch you while
you're still sedated. And
as you cry and thank me
I want you
to hold my hand
for slightly longer
than is necessary.

I want you
to be the cop
who takes me
into witness protection.
I want you to be
the one who makes up
my new name. I want you
to be the only person
in the world who knows
my location. And when,
a year later, you come
to tell me that the case is solved
I want you to lead me
to your cop car,
holding my hand
for slightly longer
than is necessary.

How to be fully-grown

In papier mâché hats for easy location
by their teachers in this museum's
sprawl, the tiny adults-in-training

are fascinated by the brilliantly-shined
museum floor, sliding along it
on their knees. This will have to be

stamped out of them, the impropriety
of dropping to the ground in the middle
of a crowded hall. As they are helped up

the giant staircase, the tiny adults-in-training,
papier-mâché-hatted, wave to us,
the fully-grown, sitting in the café. Credit-carded

we can buy cake and coffee,
but never more drop
to the ground in public

and slide on our knees
across a brilliantly-shined
museum floor.

Weighted

I am the bird at the bottom, lie on me, I beg, there is no pain in it, my loves. I am the bird at the bottom, cannot see above, further than the bird atop my chest, I breathe, and breathe best when there is something pressing down. I am the bird at the bottom, there may be anything below, there is no way for me to know unless we fall, unless we all are tumbled. But til then, I am the bird at the bottom, breathing, breathing.

Pompeii

The pills I take for panic
blanket everything and at first

I like it. Then I miss
missing you, wonder

if I can excavate
that ache. I reread

old conversations
picture

> your face
> your face
> your face

until I begin
to feel again. If

> (as turns out to be
> the case just two
> days later)

the companion is
anxiety, I'll take it, seizing

the corner of this poem
as I slip:
> my seismograph
> my pickaxe
> my safety match.

Promise

Make your daughter promise
never to do magic. Make her
swear to leave that owl alone. Tie up
her arms, shackle those legs and shroud
her sunset hair.

Make your daughter promise
never to go barefoot. Make her
swear to keep her dresses on.
Stitch up her eyelids, lace beads
tight around her unheld neck.

After she's gone, breaking
every oath she made you,
grip the beads, the lace, shackle
your neck to the sky,
and howl.

The uncertainty principle

He laughs
when I tell him,

hands outstretched
to take my parcel,

how much
I love post.

Most people
don't, he says,

and we talk
of bills. I think

I have no
fear of those. But later

I remember
the one

that came
from you a year ago,

demanding.
I dealt with it

then, and nothing
since, but still

a twinge
each time

I check.
I could seal

the hole
with tape,

brown paper,
string. But I prefer

to make friends
with uncertainty,

keep breathing,
let it all in.

The whistler

Outside, someone is whistling
as you cry. You are unbeaten,
you are unbruised. You are alone

and not unhappy for it. The cat
is a mad dashing thing. Your sadness
is a glad weight containing flavours:

>   Happiness at the happiness that was
>   Wishing and not-wishing that it might have carried on
>   Wondering how love folds into empty space

The cat is sleeping now,
the whistler has moved on.

Jerusalem stone

We meet by the wall. It's just a wall,
he says, stubbing his cigarette out
on it. Don't they know? And why

separate the sexes? Hormones,
genitalia, who cares
who fucks who or what? I have

questions, manage only to say,
Will we meet again? He glances,
grins, looks like Elvis, then like Marilyn

Monroe. I think she might
kiss me. I'm out of cigarettes,
she says. I wait by the wall, watching

the crowd slip notes in, listening
to them sing. Walking home, my lips fizz
with tar and nicotine, hips

unhooked and itching for a dance.

In tune

The novice campanologist
has been ringing
for several hours now. I listen

in my hotel room while standing
on one leg
to teach my recently-sprained ankle

where it is again. Proprioception:
our sense of ourselves
in space, why we can touch

our nose, eyes closed, how we
walk without thinking and – mostly
– do not fall. My ankle

has forgotten, in all the twist
and swell, how to chime
with the rest of me. It will take

months of practice and slow
persuasion. I wish the novice
campanologist the best. May there

always be bells to ring
in celebration, and celebration
of the silences in between.

Two nocturnes

1.

This is the day
exhaling   night

doing knee bends
in the wings   This

is the hour electric
of the empty stage

2.

I have a swimming pool
in my chest. In bed
I don't know
what to hold onto.

I have a drowning
near my heart. At night
I listen
for the sounds of rescue.

Where once Mercury had wingèd feet

now scientists hand me sandals
and an earpiece. Walk
normally, they say; then

with a slight adjustment
to my footsteps'
song, I am buoyed

lightened, as if
       gravity
           momentarily
              forgot.

Turn the dial
the other way, though
and, as if Mafia'd, I am

concrete-booted. Technology
to ground an army? No. But
if you had them, those sandals

and that earpiece, and I
held the controls, I would
root you there and kiss

and kiss you, we would need
no alteration to lift us.

Happiness

is paint. Most days I manage
a single layer of it, keeping
one eye on my mind. But then

there's you, and I
am in a factory
vat of it, up to

my neck. Enough room
for two, and enough
vats for every one of us

though the factory, size
of the universe, is hard
to find.

Tell yourself that you
are looking. Tell yourself
no wrangling over shade

or colour, gloss
or matt. Come, dip
your finger in. This

is the bright
and settled stain
you have been waiting for.

In darkness

I'm sorry for the torch not being
where I said it would be. I'm sorry
for the slip, the fall, the night
spent under stars. I'm sorry
your voice is hoarse from
shouting. The key is
not to struggle.

Notes

Sources of inspiration:

What do we do when the water rises
'Ants go marching' by Justin Nobel, *Nautilus*, July 2013.

What the choreographer knows about flight
'Rough and tumble' by Alec Wilkinson, the *New Yorker*, June 29, 2015.

Led astray by evidence
'Growing corals turn water more acidic without suffering damage' by Michael Slezak, *New Scientist*, 9 Nov 2015.

Mirrors must not be
'Antimatter' by Frank Close.

Some nature is binding
'Survivors', by Raffi Khatchadourian, the *New Yorker*, 22 Sept 2014.

Unforgotten
'They never forget: the strange gift of perfect memory' by Kayt Sukel, *New Scientist*, 15 August 2012.

For which we have no names
'How language creates your emotions' by Tiffany Watt Smith, *New Scientist*, 15 September 2015.

Missing you
'Woman of 24 found to have no cerebellum in her brain' by Helen Thompson, *New Scientist*, 10 September 2014.

Surplus, 1919

'Singled Out' by Virginia Nicholson, about the two million single women who were labelled 'surplus' and 'extra' by the press because of the lack of marriageable men after World War I.

What is it that fills us

'Gasometers: a brief history' by Daniel Johnson, *The Telegraph*, 26 Nov 2013.

Where once Mercury had wingèd feet

'Magic shoes: how to hear yourself instantly happy' by Corrine Burns, *New Scientist*, 19 Nov 2014.

Acknowledgements

Thank you to the tireless editors of the publications in which a number of these poems first appeared:
B O D Y, *The Binnacle, Butcher's Dog, 2014 Canterbury Poet of the Year anthology, The Irish Times, The Lonely Crowd, New Boots and Pantisocracies, Obsessed With Pipework, The Pickled Body*, POEM *magazine, The Rialto, Shearsman magazine, Southword, Spontaneity, Tears in the Fence, Under the Radar* and *Visual Verse*. Several of the poems were previously published in the pamphlet, *Nothing Here Is Wild, Everything Is Open* (Southword Publishing, 2016).

Thank you to Radio 3's *The Verb* for commissioning 'What is it that fills us', and to the Bristol Festival of Ideas for commissioning 'Beneath the cow' as part of the Leaving the Line Project, and to Jeremy Banning, my most excellent collaborator on that project.

Thank you to the judges of the 2017 National Poetry Competition for longlisting 'Today we have no forecast' and 'After seeing Monet's Waterlilies and then hearing the news', and to the 2017 Poetry and Psychoanalysis competition which awarded 3rd prize to 'Baby'.

An enormous thank you for advice, conversations, teaching and inspiration to:
Jill Abram, Simon Barraclough, Miranda Barnes, Clive Birnie, Mair Bosworth, Marjorie Celona, Tom Chivers, Geraldine Clarkson, Josephine Corcoran, Holly Corfield Carr, Rachael Clyne, Patrick Cotter, Adam Elgar, Alison Elgar, Pat Ferguson, Andrew Giles, Ali Griffiths, Doireann Ní Ghríofa, Fiona Hamilton, Bill Herbert, Eleanor Hooker, Kate Johnson, Victoria Kennefick, Julie Maclean,

Kathryn Maris, Jen Matthews, Joe Melia, Sharon Olds, Caleb Parkin, Pascale Petit, Jacqueline Saphra, Rachel Sara, Hilda Sheehan and Helen Taylor. Thank you to Helen Dunmore, radiant and unforgettable.

And finally, thank you to the two people without whom this book would not exist: Jane Commane, for being the best editor a writer could ever dream of, championing writers and writing with unstoppable energy and dedication; and Jo Bell, for her stoical, poetical and always joyful friendship.